ORIGAMI FUN

BIRDS

BY ROBYN HARDYMAN
AND JESSICA MOON

BELLWETHER MEDIA • MINNEAPOLIS, MN

This edition first published in 2018 by Bellwether Media, Inc.

No part of this publication may be reproduced in whole or in part without written permission of the publisher. For information regarding permission, write to Bellwether Media, Inc., Attention: Permissions Department, 5357 Penn Avenue South, Minneapolis, MN 55419.

Library of Congress Cataloging-in-Publication Data

Names: Hardyman, Robyn, author.
Title: Birds / by Robyn Hardyman.
Description: Minneapolis, MN : Bellwether Media, Inc., 2018. | Series: Express!. Origami Fun | Audience: Age 7-13. | Includes bibliographical references and index.
Identifiers: LCCN 2017000869 (print) | LCCN 2017003300 (ebook) | ISBN 9781626177086 (hardcover : alk. paper) | ISBN 9781681034386 (ebook)
Subjects: LCSH: Origami–Juvenile literature. | Birds in art–Juvenile literature.
Classification: LCC TT872.5 .H37863 2018 (print) | LCC TT872.5 (ebook) | DDC 736/.982–dc23
LC record available at https://lccn.loc.gov/2017000869

Editors: Sarah Eason and Harriet McGregor
Designers: Paul Myerscough and Jessica Moon

Printed in the United States of America, North Mankato, MN.

TABLE OF CONTENTS

ORIGAMI FUN

Origami is the art of folding paper. It has been used for hundreds of years. Origami artists make stunning animals, vehicles, and other models from a flat sheet of paper. They fold it carefully and slowly to create a work of art.

Anyone can learn the art of origami. In this book, you will learn how to make fun origami birds!

SUPPLIES
- colorful origami paper
- ruler or spoon for flattening folds
- googly eyes
- black pen
- glue
- scissors

ORIGAMI SYMBOLS
Below are key origami instruction symbols. You will find these throughout the book.

- - - - - - - - - - -	- · - · - · - · -		· · · · · · · · · · ·
Valley fold	**Mountain fold**	**Pleat fold**	**Cut line**
· · · · · · · · · · ·	⌒→	⌔→	↻
Center line	**Fold direction**	**Flip paper**	**Rotate paper**

ORIGAMI FOLDS

Valley fold
Lift the paper and bend it toward you.

Mountain fold
Bend the paper backward, away from you.

Pleat fold
First fold the paper in one direction, and then in the opposite direction.

Squash fold
Open two layers and squish them flat.

Inside reverse fold
Push the tip of the paper inward then flatten.

Bird base fold

Squash fold   Squash fold

Repeat   Lift

Squash fold   Squash fold

Kite base fold

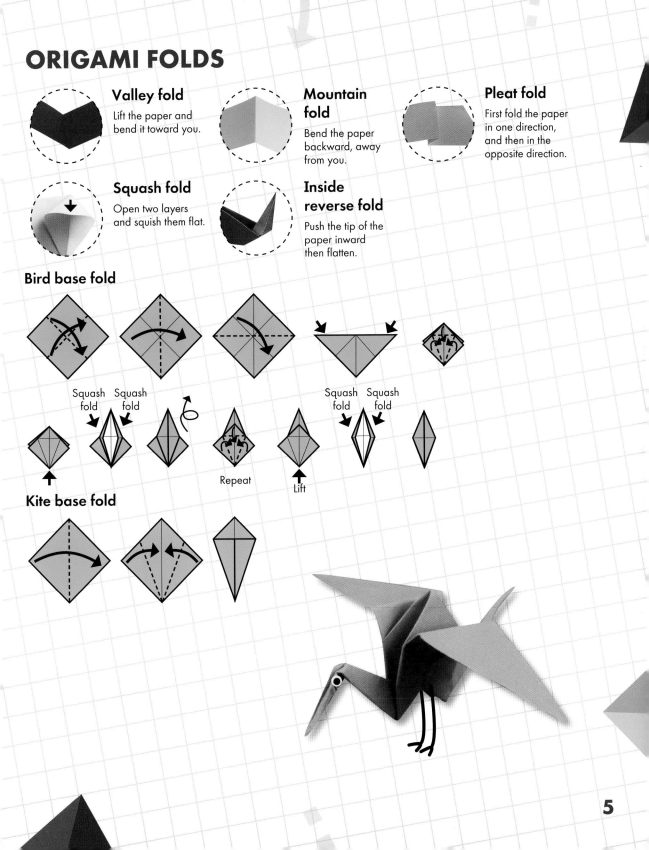

5

SWAN

Swans are large, beautiful birds with long, curved necks. They glide gracefully through rivers and lakes. They can even sleep while they float! Swans have very powerful wings and look magnificent as they fly.

Paper size:
Square sheet of origami paper,
6 x 6 inches (15 x 15 centimeters)

1

Begin with a kite base.
Turn it over.

2

Valley fold the left and right sides into the center.

3

Valley fold your model in half from bottom to top.

4

Take the upper tip, and valley fold it down to make the head.

6

5

Mountain fold the
left side back.

TIPS AND TRICKS

Make a soft crease in the paper.
Make sure it is in the right place
before you press down hard to
make a sharp crease.

6

To make the neck, pull
the head outward.

7

Rotate the model 90 degrees
clockwise. Add googly eyes and
draw wings. Widen the base,
and your swan is finished!

FANCY FLOATER!

PEACOCK

Paper size:
Square sheet of origami paper,
6 x 6 inches (15 x 15 centimeters)

The peacock is a male bird. Females are called peahens. A peacock is one of the biggest show-offs among birds! His long, bright tail feathers help him attract a **mate**. He lifts them up in a dazzling display of blue and green.

1

Begin with a kite base. Valley fold the upper left and right out to the side. Each layer should reach the edge.

2

Take the bottom point, and valley fold it up to the top.

3

Valley fold the top triangle down to the left. Make sure that the edges meet.

4

Mountain fold your model in half. Make a squash fold as you flatten it.

SQUASH FOLD

5

Make an inside reverse fold. This forms the neck.

8

6

Make another inside reverse fold. This forms the head.

7

Pleat fold the upper wing to the left. To do this, make a mountain fold on the right dotted line. Make a valley fold on the left dotted line.

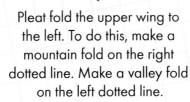

8

Your model should look like this. Turn it over.

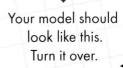

9

Pleat fold the other wing.

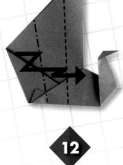

10

Open the wings.

11

Mountain fold the top point down.

12

Add googly eyes, and draw a pattern on the tail feathers. Your peacock is done!

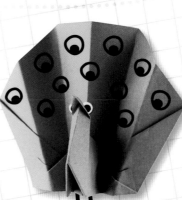

WHAT A SHOW-OFF!

CRANE

Paper size:
Square sheet of origami paper,
6 x 6 inches (15 x 15 centimeters)

Cranes are tall, graceful birds that live in large **flocks**. They have wide wings and straight beaks. These birds can fly for long distances as they search for food. They eat plants and small animals.

1

Begin with a bird base. The end that opens should point away from you. Valley fold the upper left and right sides into the center.

2

Your model should now look like this. Turn it over. Valley fold the upper left and right sides into the center.

3

Valley fold the two bottom sections out to the side. Crease them well, then unfold them.

4

Make two inside reverse folds. To do this, take the bottom tips, and pull them upward. Let the creases open. The pointed pieces will move inside the body.

5

Make an inside reverse fold on the left side. This forms the head.

TIPS AND TRICKS
The pointed end of a chopstick is useful for lifting corners and edges.

6

Valley fold the top layer. This forms the first wing.

7

Mountain fold the back layer to make the second wing.

8

Open the crane a little so it stands up. Add googly eyes and your crane is complete.

GRACEFUL BIRD!

11

OWL

Paper size:
Square sheet of origami paper,
6 x 6 inches (15 x 15 centimeters)

Some owls are tiny. Others are huge. Most are active in the nighttime. They fly silently, which helps them catch prey. Owls like to eat mice, rats, worms, and insects.

1

Begin with a bird base. The end that opens should point away from you. Valley fold the upper layer in half.

2

Your model should look like this. Turn it over. Repeat Step 1 on the other side.

3

Take the upper layer, and valley fold the left and right sides into the center.

4

Turn your model over. Repeat Step 3.

5

Valley fold the upper right layer over to the left.

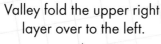

6

Pull the top triangle up and out to the right. This makes an inside reverse fold.

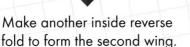

7
Valley fold the upper left layer over to the right.

8
Make another inside reverse fold to form the second wing.

9
Valley fold the top point downward.

10
Make a pleat fold.

11
Turn your model over.

12
Make two small cuts on the upper layer. These will be feathers. Cut on the dotted line at the bottom, on both layers. This makes the feet.

CUT   **CUT**

CUT

13
Fold the feathers up. Valley fold the feet back. Turn your model over.

HOO-HOO!

14
Add googly eyes, draw some feathers, and your owl is done!

13

PIGEON

Paper size:
Square sheet of origami paper,
6 x 6 inches (15 x 15 centimeters)

Pigeons are very intelligent birds. They are also awesome fliers. They have very strong wing muscles, so they can fly for a long time. They can reach speeds of 50–60 miles (80–97 kilometers) per hour! Pigeons are **herbivores** and eat seeds, fruits, and plants.

1

Valley fold the top corner to the bottom. Unfold.

2

Valley fold the right corner over to the left.

3

Next, valley fold the left side over to the right.

4

Take the upper right triangle, and fold it over to the left.

5

Valley fold your model in half from top to bottom.

6

Valley fold the upper layer to the top. This makes a wing.

7

Mountain fold the bottom layer back and up. This makes the second wing.

8

Make an inside reverse fold to form the beak.

9

Open the wings a little. Add some googly eyes, draw on feathers, and your pigeon is ready to take off!

SUPER FLIER!

DUCK

Paper size:
Square sheet of origami paper,
6 x 6 inches (15 x 15 centimeters)

Ducks love water! They live in ponds, streams, and rivers. Male ducks are called drakes, females are hens, and babies are ducklings. Their **webbed** feet work like paddles to help them swim. Their feathers are **waterproof.** Ducks quack to communicate with each other.

1

Valley fold the right corner over to the left. Unfold.

2

Valley fold the top corner down to the bottom.

3

Mountain fold the upper triangle layer back.

4

Valley fold the left and right sides into the center.

5

Next, valley fold the upper layers out to the sides.

6

Your model should look like this. Turn it over.

7

Valley fold the top left and right sides into the center. As you bring in each side, the outer edge triangles lift. Squash them back flat.

8

Your model should look like this. Mountain fold the right side back.

9

Your model should now look like this. Rotate it 90 degrees clockwise.

10

Take the left point, and fold it in toward the body. This makes an inside reverse fold.

11

Hold the tip again. Make another inside reverse fold. This forms the beak.

12

Fold the wings down, add eyes, and your duck is ready to swim.

QUACK!

SEAGULL

Paper size:
Square sheet of origami paper,
6 x 6 inches (15 x 15 centimeters)

Seagulls are large, strong birds with powerful wings. They are one of the few birds that can drink salty seawater. Seagulls are not afraid of people. Hungry seagulls sometimes swoop down to steal bites of human food. They make loud noises, too. They shriek and squawk!

1

Valley fold the paper in half both ways. Unfold.

2

Valley fold the left side toward the right.

3

Mountain fold the left side back.

4

Next, take the upper triangle, and valley fold it to the left.

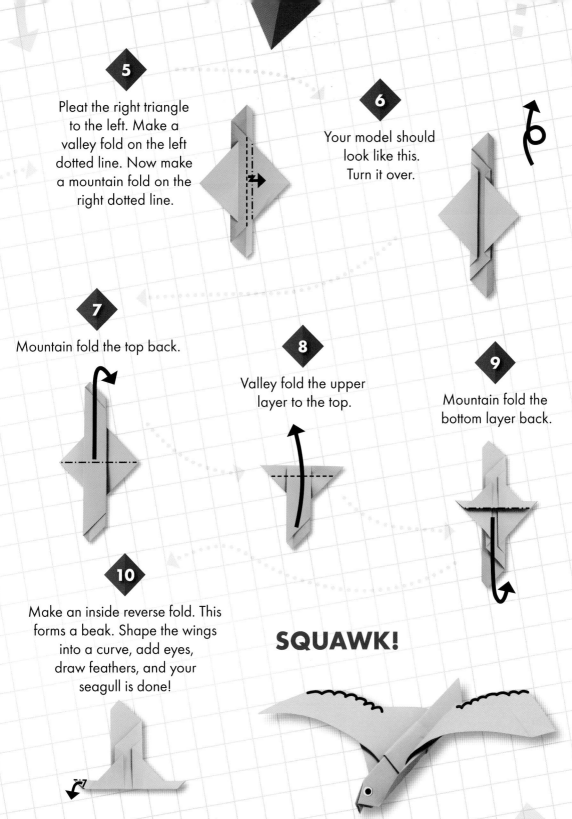

5

Pleat the right triangle to the left. Make a valley fold on the left dotted line. Now make a mountain fold on the right dotted line.

6

Your model should look like this. Turn it over.

7

Mountain fold the top back.

8

Valley fold the upper layer to the top.

9

Mountain fold the bottom layer back.

10

Make an inside reverse fold. This forms a beak. Shape the wings into a curve, add eyes, draw feathers, and your seagull is done!

SQUAWK!

KIWI

Paper size:
Square sheet of origami paper,
6 x 6 inches (15 x 15 centimeters)

Kiwis are small birds that have short brown feathers. They cannot fly, but they have an amazing sense of smell. Kiwis are **nocturnal**. They use their sense of smell to find food in the dark. They dig in the ground with their long beaks for insects and plants to eat.

1

Begin with a kite base. Valley fold the top down.

2

Valley fold the left side over to the right.

3

Your model should look like this. Turn the origami clockwise.

4

Pull the tip down. The main fold will open. Tuck the pointed piece in to make an inside reverse fold.

5

Take the inner section you just made. Make another inside reverse fold. This forms a neck that points up.

7

Add some eyes and draw on wings. Your kiwi is all set.

6

Make one more inside reverse fold. This forms the beak.

CUTE KIWI!

GLOSSARY

flocks—groups of one kind of bird

herbivores—animals that eat only plants

mate—a partner to breed with

nocturnal—active at night

waterproof—keeps water out

webbed—having toes joined by pieces of skin

TO LEARN MORE

AT THE LIBRARY

Alderfer, Jonathan. *National Geographic Kids Bird Guide of North America*. Washington, D.C.: National Geographic, 2013.

Battaglia, Vanda, and Francesco Decio. *Japanese Origami for Beginners.* North Clarendon, Vt.: Tuttle Publishing, 2015.

Stern, Joel. *My First Origami Kit*. North Clarendon, Vt.: Tuttle Publishing, 2013.

ON THE WEB

Learning more about bird origami is as easy as 1, 2, 3.

1. Go to www.factsurfer.com.

2. Enter "bird origami" into the search box.

3. Click the "Surf" button, and you will see a list of related web sites.

With factsurfer.com, finding more information is just a click away.

INDEX